How to Have Success and Still Keep Your Chilhood

Caleb Maddix

Book Cover Design: Caleb Maddix

Editing: Amy Kochek

Printing and/or ordering information:

amazon.com

Table of Contents

1

Your Figure Out What Childhood Means

WHHHHHAAAATTTTTTSSSSSSSS UP, MADDIX ADDICTS‼ I am back with another book, and I am about to drop the fire in this one. Obviously, the other ones were filled with fire as well, but this one is going to take you to another level. Get ready because I am about to destroy some myths about childhood.

If you were to ask someone what it means to be a kid, I'm sure you would hear many different answers. To some people, being a child means having fun, making mistakes, hanging out with friends, buying toys, playing video games, going to school, and using a cell phone all day. All of these may be part of being a child, but that doesn't mean that you can't do more, be more, and have more.

Age is just a number that defines how long you live, but you shouldn't let it define *how* you live. You may not know this, but years ago, the images of childhood were quite different. Television shows would broadcast images of kids and teenagers that were coming home, doing their homework, playing outside, and then going to bed. On the weekends, these same kids and teens were having sleepovers, pulling pranks, watching movies, and eating junk food.

While there is nothing wrong with these images, and most of them still exist, there is a different kind of image that is being broadcast all over the media. Childhood is no longer that simple. With the invention of the cellphone, YouTube, Facebook, Instagram, and Twitter, there are so many different opportunities and lifestyles that are presented to kids.

Wait, before we move forward, I want you to let something sink in. Did you know that people used to live without YouTube (gasp), Facebook (face palm), Instagram (shock emoji), and cellphones (scream in horror)? Let's have a moment of silence for all those deprived kids that had to suffer through these terrible years. Whew, now let's move forward in gratitude that we are alive in this amazing time filled with wonderful technology.

Years ago, childhood looked a lot different because kids didn't have what we have today. Their lifestyle fit the society they lived in. This means that we are redefining what childhood means right now. We are not trying to just fit in. We aren't willing to settle for what everyone says we should become. Remember, we aren't average, but we are SAVAGE.

Looking through the accomplishments of many of my readers is astonishing because some of you have achieved goals that adults only dream about. The technology world allows us to do things that our parents couldn't even imagine. Because of this, we are able to do things that may seem unbelievable to adults or average kids.

Your childhood doesn't have to be filled with irresponsibility and ignorance. It can be filled with big goals and focused vision. You may be writing a book, building a business, traveling around the world, or speaking in front of thousands of people.

If you guys remember, I told you the story about receiving the opportunity to speak with Gary Vaynerchuck in Australia. It was one of the most life changing experiences. First of all, it was my first time traveling out of the country. Imagine this. Here is this 14-year-old kid boarding a plane to fly overseas and speak in front of crowd with over 600 people. Not only that, I was speaking with some of the most influential business minds in the world.

Needless to say, I was beyond excited. While my dad and I were on the plane, I couldn't stop smiling. After a year and a half, my goal of speaking with Gary V. had been achieved.

To some, a 14-year old's dream to speak with one of the greatest business influencers would seem, "cute." I mean, I was a kid, right? Kids are supposed to just focus on their grades in school and having fun. They aren't supposed to have big dreams like this. And if they do, they are supposed to be accomplished later in life, right? Wrong!

I am thankful that my dad understood that you don't live your childhood years irresponsibly and then start planning once you graduate high school. He allowed me to dream big, work hard, and accomplish goals that may not seem age appropriate to others. However, I had to remember that I wasn't living my life for other people or for the definition of childhood that society was trying to feed me.

As the plane landed in Australia, it felt like there was a little man in my stomach doing back flips. I wasn't nervous, it was more of an overwhelming excitement. My dreams were coming to life in front of my face, and I wanted to experience every moment of it.

When we arrived at the speaking venue, I was greeted by the organizer of the event. They brought me back stage to a room that was reserved for the speakers. There were bottles of water, food, and comfortable seats in the room. As the room filled, I realized that I was surrounded by extremely successful people. This opportunity would not be wasted, so I introduced myself to almost every person in the room. I asked questions, listened, and requested their best advice.

For 30 minutes, I learned as much as I could. Then, I turned around and saw Gary V. enter the room. It was an emotional moment, not filled with tears, but extreme happiness. I watched almost every one of Gary V.'s videos, and I couldn't wait to ask him for his best advice. Though it was only a moment, I was able to speak with and shake Gary V.'s hand.

Remember, I accomplished ALL of this, and I was only 14 years old. My energy and confidence were high as I walked onto the stage. It was such an incredible moment, and the audience responded well to my keynote. After the speech, I asked the audience if they had any questions.

A young lady stood up and after she started talking, it was clear that she did not have a question. She was upset. She told me that she felt sorry for me because I was losing my childhood. She said, while I may have success, I lost the ability to spend my early years as a child. The responsibilities I had were too great, and it was clear that I couldn't just be a kid. She then continued by saying that her child was much better off because he could play and relax while I spent my time working like an adult.

After her rant, she took her seat again. The room was quiet as everyone looked back at me to give her a response. I was stunned, and I didn't really know what to say. Once I gathered my thoughts, I responded in kindness, but the truth is, she was completely wrong.

Her perception of childhood was much different than mine. Based on her comments, she believed that being a child meant not working too hard and having fun. In her eyes, traveling, speaking, and writing books were viewed as an attack on my childhood.

This was not the first time that I've heard adults give their opinions about my life's choices. My dad and I have received many phone calls, text messages, and DM's from adults that make judgements based on how I live my life. The truth is, even though I have many supporters and followers, I also have a large number of haters that aren't patting me on the back and telling me what a great job I'm doing. Their definition of childhood directly conflicts with my definition. In most cases, they are echoing the opinions of the young woman in Australia. They think I'm, "missing out" on my childhood.

Here's the great part about this. That is ok. It's ok that people disagree with my life and decisions. It's ok if people believe that I'm too young to be doing what I'm doing. That's their opinion, and guess what, their opinion is none of my business.

After the young lady gave her opinion in Australia, I didn't go home and cry. I didn't start changing my goals and dreams because she disagreed. Her opinion was none of my business. If she believed that childhood meant fun, conventional school, sports, relaxing, and lack of responsibility, then that is her business. She has a right to not only have her opinion, but to raise her kids based on her definition of childhood. At the same time, I have the right to define what childhood means for me and live my life without apology or explanation to other people.

Even though my life may be strange to some or appear to be too stressful, the reality is that I love my life. While my friends are watching YouTube sensation, Jake Paul, I have been able to hang out with Jake Paul. While my friends are watching TV, I get to be on TV. While my friends are making goals, I'm living out my goals. While my friends are sharing viral videos, I'm making viral videos. While my friends are reading books, I'm writing and publishing books. While my friends . . . well, you get the point.

I'm not listing these things because I'm trying to brag, (even though all this stuff has been pretty awesome), I'm showing you that success doesn't have to just be dedicated to adults or a select group of people. It is available for anyone that is hungry enough to go get it. My life is a redefinition of the old, worn out view of childhood that says the average is the norm. I want my life to defeat average and proclaim savage.

At the same time, people are only able to see a portion of my life. This means that opinions of others can only be based on their limited perception from what they see on Facebook, Instagram and YouTube. Yeah, I travel around the world, meet celebrities, speak in front of large audiences, and make good money. However, my life is properly balanced with fun and play.

My work day is planned by actions. This means that I focus on working on one task at a time. The agenda could include filming, writing, creating content, or a list of other demands for the day.

After an action is complete, I then take a break. During this time, I make sure that I'm not doing anything that surrounds my work. Break time can include going on social media, taking a walk around the block, talking on the phone, or leisure reading.

A proper balance between work and play is something that my dad has stressed ever since I can remember. Every day, we try to incorporate fun activities such as rollerblading, tennis, hoverboarding, and baseball.

Some of my work days can be intense due to the workload. On one such day, I remember walking away from my desk to go find my dad. Once I found him, I said that I needed a break from work for a while. Even though my dad knew we had some deadlines to meet, he understood the importance of balance. We went home, changed, and spent 2 hours on the basketball court. That time away from work allowed me to have fun, relax, and recharge.

Remember, we aren't trying to live an average childhood, we are living a savage childhood. What does a savage childhood look like? You get to decide.

My savage childhood looks different than any of my friends, but that is ok.

My definition of my savage childhood is to work my face off to pursue my dreams and goals while having fun, making money, and changing the world for the better. This definition doesn't rob me of my childhood. It brings new life to it.

I have an unbelievable work ethic, which just means that I believe that hard work pays off. My success at a young age did not come from luck or chance. It came through hard work, consistency, and focus. There were many sacrifices that I had to make, but one sacrifice I didn't make was to give up my childhood. I just redefined it.

Now, Maddix Addicts, this is my challenge for you. It's now time to define what childhood means to you. You are savage, so you may not be able to look at your other friends or classmates to find the definition. Using everything you are learning from my books about being a savage kid, define what kind of savage kid you are going to be and live it every single day.

2

Say No to the Good so You Can Say Yes to the Best

I magine coming home from school and you are starving. I mean you are so hungry that you can eat a cow. Ok, you probably wouldn't eat a whole cow, but you could eat a lot of stuff. Once you get home, you look through the cabinets and just start eating snacks. You fill up on pop tarts, chips, and soda. Once you are done stuffing your face, you sit down to start your homework. An hour later, your mom comes home with your favorite meal.

She said she knew you would be hungry, so she went and picked it up just for you. Imagine how bummed you would be. This delicious food is sitting right in front of you just waiting to be destroyed, but you can't eat it because you filled up on snacks. If you had just waited a little longer, you would be eating your favorite meal, but now all you have is a stomachache.

If you had said no to your good snacks, you could have said yes to the best food. Being a savage kid means that you are going to have to say no to the good so you can wait for the best and say yes when it comes. Even though playing all day, sleeping in, and hanging out all the time with friends sounds great, you may have to say no. You must say no to those good things so that you can find success with the best things like living off a schedule, waking up early, and working on your business.

When I first started playing baseball, I wasn't good at all. I know this will come as a shock to all of you, but in my younger years, I was shorter, slower, and weaker than most of my teammates. These facts didn't discourage me, but they motivated me to push myself to become better. In a short time, I became one of the best players on the team. Despite my height and weight, I played better than some of my teammates that doubled me in size.

13

On one weekend, we were playing an important tournament. That Friday, we played four long games that started in the morning and lasted until later that afternoon. We won all four of the games, which meant that we were going to play in the championship the next day. To celebrate, the team decided to have a pool party. Everyone was excited about our wins that day, and they were ready to relax by the pool.

The pool party sounded fun, but I knew that we still had the championship game to play the next day. I told my coaches and teammates that instead of going to the party, I was going to go to the batting cages and just hit. My plan sounded ridiculous to my coaches and teammates. They said, "We have played all day. Just come to the pool party, so you can have fun and goof off for a bit. You don't need extra practice. You are working too hard."

Despite their pushback, I went to the batting cages anyway. For hours, I hit ball after ball. My focus was so intense that I lost track of time. Long after the sun went down, I was still at the batting cages, hitting. To make sure that I didn't become exhausted, I would take breaks in between my hitting to watch YouTube videos of other baseball players' swings and study the videos I was filming of my own swing.

While I was working, my energy was high, and I kept a positive attitude. Audiobooks, music, and motivational speeches played in the background to keep me focused. My dad and I even played catch during some of my break times. At 10:00 pm, it was time for me to pack up and head home.

Once I arrived home, my body was tired, but my mind was alert and ready for the next game. There was not a moment that I thought about the pool party or the fun I may be missing out on. All I could think about was performing my best for the next game.

When my dad and I arrived at the field the next day, I collected my gear and met my teammates and coaches in the dugout. They were laughing and talking about the events that occurred at the party the night before. One of my friends told me that I really missed out on a fun party, and I should have been there. Even though their stories sounded great,

I had no regrets about my choice to continue practicing instead of going to the party.

My decision paid off. I played one of my best games that season. The hours I spent practicing my swing showed on the field, and my hustle and focus were at an all-time high. We won the final game and my teammates and I celebrated. It was such a great feeling. Moments later, we gathered on the field for the awards ceremony.

After we settled down, there was one more trophy. It was the MVP award. The head coach picked up the large, gold trophy and presented it to me. I was so excited. Out of all the outstanding players on the all-star teams, I was chosen as the most valuable player.

When I went up to get the award, my teammates surrounded me and we all started jumping up and down and cheering. This was one of the most memorable moments of my life. After the celebration, we all walked back to the dugout. My coaches came up to me to shake my hand and tell me how proud they were of me. Right before I reached the dugout, I saw my dad come rushing towards me. He gave me one of the tightest hugs and told me what a huge moment this was. Not only did he tell me he was proud of my award, he also said that he was prouder of the work that I did when no one else was watching. I chose the best when others chose the good.

We hung out a little while after the game until one of the parents told us that we were going to have a big party to celebrate the team's accomplishment. With the big game complete, I was now ready to relax and have a good time with my friends.

Sometimes reaching success and accomplishing big goals takes a great deal of sacrifice. I had to sacrifice the day I decided to go to the batting cages instead of the party. It was an unpopular decision and most people were against it. However, I knew that I didn't just want to play an average game, I wanted to play a savage game. This meant that I had to make a hard decision, which in the end, worked in my favor.

Remember, the road to success is paved with sacrifices. It won't be easy. If it were easy, there would be a traffic jam on this road. The truth is, it can be a lonely journey at times because everyone won't be making the same decisions as you. That is ok.

This is where mental toughness must come in. If I had decided to go to the party as opposed to the batting cages, I might not have been MVP. I may have had fun at the party, but my focus and attitude may have been off the next day. The result of this choice could have been a loss for my team or someone else winning the MVP award.

In life, there will be choices that you must make. Each choice will cost you something. If you choose to work an extra hour on your business, you will have to give up that extra hour of TV you wanted to watch. The same can be said if you choose to watch an extra hour of TV as opposed to working on your business. You just must decide which cost is worth paying.

Saying no to the good can be painful because it may be something that we really want to do. The only thing that will help you do this is mental toughness. Realize that to get the best, you must work the best. Big dreams require big sacrifices, and those sacrifices will pay off. Trust me.

I've had to say no to a great deal of, "good," but it has allowed the best to continue to flow into my life. My friends were riding their bikes, but I was reading a success book. My friends were posting selfies on social media, but I was posting a motivational video. My friends were spending their money on video games and clothes, but I was saving my money to invest into my business. My friends were going on dates, but I was in business meetings.

I believe in sacrifice, and I've made some big ones in my short life. However, if it weren't for these sacrifices, you wouldn't be reading a book written by me. You wouldn't be watching the inspirational videos I post on my social media. Without sacrifice, I would be an average kid living an average life.

A year ago, I received a tweet from an old friend from school. She said, "Caleb, you are so lucky." This tweet upset me so much because nothing in my life has come because of luck. I've worked for everything I've achieved. I wasn't born into a wealthy family that gave me a pile of money. My baby clothes weren't made of gold, and I didn't grow up in a room filled with toys and gadgets.

Do you want to know why I was invited to Arnold Schwarzenegger's house? Because I worked for it. Do you want to know why I owned my first business at the age of 14? Because I worked for it. Do you want to know why I made over $100,000 at the age of 14? Because I worked for it. I could obviously go on, but you get the point. Luck plays no role in success but sacrifice and discipline does.

Learning how to say no to the good takes some time and focus. Some of you may be reading this and thinking that I should have just gone to the pool party. Let's go back to goals for a minute. In my book, *Keys to Success 2.0*, we discussed goals and made a list of them. When you have specific goals, you have to understand the cost to achieve those goals.

When I played baseball, I had many goals that I wanted to achieve. Because I wrote my goals every day and stayed focused on them, I knew I had to say no to the good, which was the pool party, to say yes to the best, which was the MVP. If you are constantly working towards your goals, you will know when it is appropriate to say no to the good so you can say yes to the best. You will know when to work and when to play.

I went to the pool party after the championship game was complete. My goal was completed, and I knew it was time for me to relax as opposed to work. I understood the timeline of my goal, which meant I knew when it was time to push and then back off.

Professional weightlifters go through seasons that are matched with fitness goals. The winter months are referred to as the bulk (get bigger) season. This is when weight lifters focus on eating more to gain mass and strength. During this time, they not only eat more food, but they also lift heavier weights.

On the other hand, the summer months are referred to as the lean (get smaller) season. During this time, they eat less calories and lift lighter weight. Doing this allows their body to become lighter because they are cutting back on the amount and types of food they eat.

Let's say that a weightlifter went to a party in July. The food choices included pizza, chips, cake, and soda. He was absolutely starving and all of his friends were eating the food. No one would know that eating the food would be hurting his goals but him. He could easily fill up his stomach with junk food, but it would come at the cost of his goals. Remember, every choice has a cost.

If he decides to pass on the junk food, his friends might make fun of him or tell him that he should enjoy himself at the party. However, he will stay on track with his goal. He must decide to say no to the momentary good so he can say yes to the best.

Kobe Bryant, a retired NBA player, said that for 45 weeks of the year, he was one of the most focused drill sergeants when it came to playing basketball. He said that he was one of the hardest working basketball players on the planet. Then he said, for the 7 weeks during the off season, he allowed himself to become lazy so his body and mind could rest. Once those weeks were up and regular season began, he picked back up and started again.

Guys, sacrifice and discipline are required on this journey towards success. I will say this again - it will not be easy. Stay focused on your goals and your season of sacrifice will become easier. If you made a goal to write a book by the end of the year, you are going to have to make sacrifices to reach this goal. You must say no to hanging out with friends all the time, talking on the phone, going to the movies every weekend, or spending all your time on social media.

When you reach your goal and hold your published book in your hand, you can take some time to relax and celebrate. In that moment, all the good that you gave up will fade into the background and all you will see is the BEST that you chose despite the sacrifice.

3

Find Friends That Have the Same Mission as You

I n Australia, there was a baby kangaroo named, Dusty. A friendly family rescued him shortly after his mother died. Immediately, Dusty became a part of the family, but he spent most of his time with the two family dogs.

Dusty spent his days following the dogs around, sleeping with them, and running around the back yard with them. After a while, Dusty started to copy the dogs' behaviors. He would hop towards his human family and request to be rubbed by nudging their hands.

His behaviors looked so much like the dogs' that the family believed that Dusty thought he was a dog.

Years later, he still lives with the family and still acts just like the other two dogs. Even when he had the opportunity to go back into the wild to join other kangaroos, he stayed at the house with the dogs.

When I came across this story, I thought it was amazing. How often do you see people walking their pet kangaroos around the block? Probably never. Kangaroos are not house pets, and they don't usually act like dogs. In this case, Dusty started acting like a dog because he spent all of his time around dogs. He started to pick up their habits and behaviors because it was all he knew. He didn't spend any time with other kangaroos, so he didn't have the same behaviors that those kangaroos had.

Dusty could teach all of us an important lesson. We become who we spend the most time with. In fact, John Maxwell, a popular motivational speaker once said, "You are the average of the 5 people you spend the most time with." That is powerful. If you are spending time with 5 average kids, you will stay average. If you are spending time with 1 savage kid and 4 other average kids, you will still be average.

But if you are spending time with 5 savage kids, you can't help but be savage as well.

Right now, some of you may be like Dusty. You proclaim that you want to be a savage kid, but you are hanging out with average kids. A person's success can be predicted based on the people they spend the most time with.

Friends are important. We all need them and hopefully, we all have them. Friends can encourage us, make us laugh, and entertain us when we are bored. Successful kids make sure that the friends they choose have the same mission as them. For instance, if your goal is to make straight A's on your report card, it would not be a good idea to hang out with a bunch of kids who get F's on their report card. If you want to be business owner, it would be a good idea to hang out with friends who have big dreams just like you. You want to be around other kids who are positive and hard working so they will encourage you and make sure you are making good decisions.

In order to find friends that have the same mission, you must know your mission. Since you are part of the Maddix Addicts community, your mission is to be average and not savage. We hate the word normal and redefine society's view of successful kids. Most importantly, we are changing the world, one successful kid at a time.

This is a pretty awesome mission, right? The key to remember is that a mission isn't just a group of motivational words that we say. Our mission is what drives us. It is what wakes us up in the morning and motivates us to work our faces off. It is what helps us say no to the good and yes to the best. Most importantly, our mission guides us in determining our close friendships.

I've never really been an average, normal kid. Ever since I can remember, I always had a passion and drive to become successful in whatever I did. Because of this, I had a hard time fitting in. Don't get me wrong, I had friends. During my years in school, most of my friends were in the popular crowd. Even though I had friends, I didn't really feel like I could connect with any of them. Their goals and mindset were different than mine.

When I started my own business and began networking with other entrepreneurial minded people, my environment changed. I was being introduced to people like me. There was nothing necessarily wrong with the friends I had in school, but they had a totally different focus than I had. Keeping these friends close became a struggle because we were going in different directions.

About a year ago, my dad and I were looking for someone to come help us with marketing. I was on Facebook one night and watched a video about a contest Grant Cardone hosted. Whoever made the most creative sales pitch won the contest. When I watched the video, I saw the winner of the contest that appeared to be around my age.

His sales method and work ethic interested me so much that I decided to contact him. That initial contact led to an arrangement that allowed him to come work with our team for a month. The first night he arrived, we spent most of the time talking about marketing strategies, business ideas, and creative ways to make money.

Our values and personalities were so similar that we stayed up until early in the morning. For the next month, our friendship grew because the foundation was based upon a similar passion. We both had a strong drive to succeed and to help others do the same. In our free time, we didn't play video games or watch TV, instead we researched other successful people, read success books, and collaborated with other young entrepreneurs.

The month that he stayed with us in Florida was quite memorable. After many years, I felt like I finally found a close friend that I could connect with. As I said earlier, I've always had friends, but finding someone that shared similar interests as me was a challenge. This guy just got it. He was savage and refused to settle for average.

His commitment to excellence and unbelievable work ethic made it easy for us to connect. Even though he lives far away, we have stayed closely connected. The foundation of our friendship is built on a similar mission, which is why our bond remains strong.

Now, I don't want you to think that I don't have fun with my friends. While he stayed in Florida, we made time for breaks from our work. Remember, it is important to have a balance between work and play.

We played beach volleyball, watched movies, and went sightseeing in London.

The difficulty I had with finding like-minded friends to connect with was one of the reasons I started helping kids find other successful kids. I didn't want kids that were hungry for success to have to frustrate themselves in the search for close friends that shared their mission. This is why I'm inviting you with me on a journey towards success.

Guys, you don't have to go through the same pains that I did to find mission minded friends. The Maddix Addict community is a place for you to connect with the other people so that you can encourage, challenge, learn, grow, and have crazy fun doing it.

I'm going to give you all two challenges. The first challenge is to spend time reading my books and taking notes. Share the content with friends and other kids that you want to join you on your success journey. These actions will help you build relationships with the other members so you are not trying to go through this process alone. My journey to success started alone, but I've brought a couple other people along with me. It has made a huge difference.

The other challenge is to get one of your friends to read my books with you. One of my readers encouraged 4 of his friends at school to join him with reading my books. Once they started meeting, they started a mini success group. After school, they gathered together and went over the book and some of my videos. These kids are challenging one another, discussing what they are learning, and sharing their strategies for application.

This is so powerful. I know that all of you are learning so much from the books, videos, and content. How much more would you benefit from sharing the awesome content of this book with someone else? This is such an easy way to find friends that share the same mission as you.

When you start to get your friends onboard, I want you to share what you all have been learning together. Use your social media as a place to report what your group has been doing. Use the hashtags #missionminded #MaddixAddict. I can't wait to hear about the progress of your group and the memories that you all will make together. Most importantly, you will have friends that allow you to share in the fun and learning opportunities together.

4

Make Work Fun

Have you ever been in school and the teacher is talking, but you are completely zoned out? You know you should be working, but you are sitting at your desk, daydreaming about being anywhere but school. This can be true for other tasks that we may not find enjoyable. For those of you that are in sports, you may hate practice because it can be boring and hard sometimes. What about homework time? Do you hate it? When it is time to read, do you absolutely dread it?

These negative emotions and lack of focus can happen when we don't find the fun in our work. I know some of you may be thinking that work and fun cannot be put in the same sentence. But you are completely wrong. Work can be fun, but it is up to you to make it that way.

One of the first problems with making work fun is that we think the word, "work," is a negative word. When we hear that word, thoughts of boredom or pain come to our mind.

Much of what we have to conquer in life starts in our mind, so that is the first place that we are going to start. Make up in your mind that when you hear the word, "work," you are going to replace that negative thought with a positive one. Let's say that you have a ton of homework to complete. I'm not telling you to jump for joy that you'll have to do a Math worksheet that will take you 30 minutes to complete. What I am telling you to do is to find the positive point in your work. You will remember this strategy in the positive book.

Before you start your homework, find a comfortable space that is away from distractions. It is important that your environment fits your work style. For instance, I knew this guy that didn't like to sit on regular chairs. He preferred to sit on a huge ball that is used for exercising. Also, he only liked instrumental music playing in the background while he did his work. This environment may not work for you, which is why you must find what type of environment makes it easier for you to focus on work and have fun in the process.

Remember, I told you guys that I was one of the worst players on my baseball team, but I had a goal to get on the All-Star team. That meant that I was going to have to work extremely hard to get there. One of the main tools that is used to improve baseball skills is drills. The problem with this is that I didn't really like drills. They could be boring sometimes. Hitting drills meant that I would simply hit one ball after the other. It was hard for me to get excited about something that I thought was boring.

My dad helped me overcome the mental block I seemed to have with getting motivated to do baseball drills. We stopped calling them drills and started making games out of everything we did. He rarely had me do batting practice or just throwing ground balls to me. To improve my fielding skills, my dad used something called a reaction ball. It is a ball that has all these rubber spikes coming out of it. When it bounces on the ground, it starts to go all over the place. My dad would throw it high up in the air and let it drop. I would then have to try to get the ball as quickly as I could while it bounced.

Another game my dad and I used to play was called turn around reaction. I would have my back to my dad and he would hit the ball. Then he would say, "turn," and I would have to field the ball as quickly as possible. Then, my dad would also throw the ball really high in the air, and if I caught 7 out of 10, my dad would give me a prize. There were countless other games that we played together that were work, but they didn't feel like it.

When my dad coached my baseball team, our practices looked very different from other teams. Most people believed that to get better, they had to do repeated drills. My dad didn't use that strategy. He made our practices fun and always incorporated some form of competition. The winner always received a prize at the end. In addition to that, our team played a game of football before every baseball game. Other teams thought this was strange, but we used it as a warm up.

That year, our team won the most games. Our energy was high, and we maintained positive attitudes. Laughter was a familiar sound because we were always having a good time even though we were working at the same time.

I took this same mentality and mindset into my business. Each day, I spend a great deal of my time working, but it doesn't feel like work. I wake up with enthusiasm and excitement for the day. My work space fits my personality. During the work day, I play Christmas music in the background because I love it. My dad and I tell jokes and laugh in the office. Also, during my breaks, I go on walks and play tennis.

When it is time for my dad and I to do sales calls, we make it a game. We keep a tally to see how many calls we can make in an hour and how many sales we close. The competition makes work seem more like a game, which builds the energy in the office.

Like I said in a previous chapter, I take breaks after I complete a task. During these breaks, I incorporate activities that I enjoy. I like to listen to Christmas music while I work. I know that may sound weird, but Christmas is the best time of year, in my opinion. There is something about it that brings such upbeat attitudes and an overall sense of love and giving. Anytime I hear a Christmas song, my mood is immediately lifted.

I also enjoy telling jokes, going on walks, and playing tennis. Enthusiasm is essential during your work time because it allows you to stay focused and positive. If you are tired, upset, or negative, you will struggle finding enjoyment in your work. This will affect your productivity. Every activity that I choose for my breaks keeps my enthusiasm and positivity up. Also, they fit my personality as well. My health is important to me, so I incorporate actions that keep my body moving.

Making work fun is a high priority for me. I'm intense with everything that I do, but I'm not tense. Meaning, I put 100% into my life, business, relationships, and health, but I am not so tense that

I don't know how to have fun in the process. Remember this, Maddix Addicts, be intense, but don't be tense.

There are times when I log into my social media and I become immediately frustrated by some of the posts that I see. It may shock you to discover that most of these posts are written by adults. I see people say things like, "I hate Mondays," "Only 1 more day until the weekend," "I can't wait until vacation." While the desire to have days off or take a break from work is not bad, the idea that work is the opposite of fun can be really damaging.

If you start to believe that your career or job is simply something you do to make money whether you are having fun or not, you have missed the point. You know one way to keep success and still be a kid? Never stop being a kid. What do I mean by that? Never stop having fun. Never stop telling jokes and laughing. Never stop playing games. Never stop appreciating the small things.

Sometimes adults lose an element of fun when they grow up. They start believing that working means you have to be bored and miserable for 5 days a week, celebrate during the weekend, and hate the beginning of the week. What a sad life! If you only have 2 days a week that you are happy and having fun, then there is a problem. You should be having fun and enjoying life every day of the week, whether you are working or taking a break from your work.

Google is one of the best employers in the world. People spend years trying to get a job there. Why? Because Google has created a workplace that allows its employees to accomplish great things and have fun at the same time. If you were to look up pictures of what the Google building looks like, it would appear to be a huge adult playground. Obviously, the adults are not spending all day on slides and swings. However, they do take breaks throughout the day that involve fun activities such as video games, ping pong, and foosball.

Google's success as a brand and a workplace shows the importance of balancing work and play into your day. Even the way the building looks, motivates the employees to keep positive attitudes and smiles on their faces throughout the work day.

Now it is your turn to determine how you will incorporate fun into your work and break times. All of this will depend on your personality and what works best for you. For example, you may create a game show out of your homework, set a timer for each question you have to answer, play upbeat music in the background, or pretend that you are giving a speech about the content you have to study.

Whatever you decide, make sure that you are in an environment that allows you to feel comfortable and at ease. If you complete work in your bedroom, clean up your room. A dirty room can make it more difficult to concentrate. Put up pictures, art work, or motivational quotes that inspire you. I painted my room bright blue, put up letters on my wall that said, "Work Your Face Off," and posted my goals throughout my bedroom. Each time I went in there to start working, I felt comfortable and motivated to begin my work. I sat at a clean desk in a tidy room. This helped me maintain a greater focus and ultimately made work more fun.

Once you arrange your workspace, I want you to take a picture of it and post it on social media with

#MaddixAddict. Also, take a picture of yourself doing a fun activity during your work or break time. Post it on your page with #MakeWorkFun. I can't wait to see what you guys come up with. Don't become the type of kid or adult that lives for the weekend because you are bored out of your mind during the weekdays. Celebrate your life and create fun in everything you do.

5

Wherever You Are at Be There

One of my all-time favorite songs is called, "Don't Blink." The reason that I enjoy this song so much is because I connect to the message found within the lyrics. Anytime I find my life going by too quickly or when I feel like I'm not living in the moment, I listen to this song to remind me that life is very short.

The writer of this song is remembering a time when he was watching an interview on TV between a news reporter and a 102-year-old man. Since he was a much older man that obviously had many valuable life experiences, the news reporter asked him what was the secret to life. I always find it interesting when people ask that question because it seems like we are all trying to figure that out. In our pursuit of success, love, health, and wealth, we are all really trying to figure out what is the secret to living the best life.

Well, the old man gave a simple yet difficult answer. He said, "Don't blink." I'm going to share the chorus of the song so his response makes a little bit more sense. "Don't blink/Just like that you're six years old and you take a nap and you/Wake up and you're twenty-five/and your high school sweetheart becomes your wife/Don't blink/You might miss your babies growing like mine did/Turning into moms and dads next thing you know/your 'better half' of fifty years is there in bed/And you're praying God takes you instead/Trust me friend a hundred years goes faster than you think/So don't blink."

Some people don't learn this valuable lesson until it is way too late. Second, minutes, hours, days, months, and years go by so quickly. You only get to live one day at a time, and once those days are gone, you cannot get them back. Even God himself cannot give you time back. There are so many things that you can get back, but time is not one of them.

That's why it is so important to value each moment of this journey. Successful kids can be busy. There is nothing wrong with being busy, but don't miss out on special memories because you are so obsessed and forget to enjoy the moment. If you are with your friends, be with your friends. Laugh, play, joke, whatever you all are doing – enjoy the moment. Don't think about your homework, business deal, or writing a book. Just be there with your friends.

If you are having a family dinner, don't get on your phone and text your friends, check your social media, or play games. Be with your family. Talk to each other, tell stories, and create memories. When successful kids don't enjoy moments, they miss out on experiences, relationships, and memories.

A couple of years ago, my mom purchased tickets to Busch Gardens, which is a local theme park here is Florida. Tourists from all over the world come to visit this place. It is actually pretty cool. They have a zoo, roller coasters, games, live shows, and restaurants. I knew we were going to spend all day at the park, so I made sure to get all my work done the day before so I could enjoy my time with my mom.

Once I arrived, I became super excited because I love roller coasters. As my mom and I walked around the park, we spent time talking with one another and enjoying the sights. We laughed and screamed during the rides. It was really great. However, after about an hour, I started to become distracted. I don't know where the thought came from, but all of a sudden, I remembered that I didn't post one of my videos on YouTube the night before.

Since social media is such an important aspect of my business, I spend a great deal of time doing videos and posts on my pages. It is the way I connect with my community and share life-changing content.

After the thought came into my head, I could not think of anything else. I tried to distract myself with conversation and the surrounding environment, but my mind would just go right back to that video. Instead of talking with my mom, I started scrolling through my phone. While we waited to get on rides, my eyes remained glued on my phone screen.

I stopped focusing on where I was at and who I was with and started focusing on work that needed to be accomplished. My mom could sense my distraction and made a few comments to me. She asked me to get off my phone, so I did. Even though I ended up putting my phone away, I spent the rest of the day thinking about that video. Because my focus shifted to other things, distracting thoughts entered my mind.

I was no longer just thinking of that one YouTube video. I then started thinking of videos that I wanted to post of Facebook and an idea for an Instagram post. On the way back to my house, my mom mentioned that she had a great time, but she wished that I hadn't spent so much time on my phone. After she made that comment, I reflected over the day. While I didn't realize it at the time, I felt like I cheated myself out of the experience because I wasn't enjoying the moment.

My mind and heart were somewhere else when they should have been at Busch Gardens with my mom. While I may have the opportunity to go back to Busch Gardens with my mom, I will never have that moment back again. It is gone, and I didn't treat it as sacred as I should have. There will come a time when

I won't be able to spend time with my mom in the way I do now.

One day, I will be grown up with a family and children of my own. I won't be able to spend the day talking and laughing with just my mom. That was the moment I was gifted, but I didn't treat it like a gift. I treated it like a chore.

Guys, I think the iPhone is one of the greatest inventions ever made. I also believe that social media has completely changed the way we do business, relationships, and even life. I personally benefit from technology and social media because they have helped me build a business and put it on a larger platform. And by the way, if you are an Android user and don't own any Apple products, get help now! LOL!

The problem is, something that was created for us to use as a tool to enhance life can be used to replace life. We can spend so much time on our phones and social media posting and taking pictures of our lives that we actually stop really living and enjoying the moments of our lives.

Not only that, our own minds can keep us from staying in the moment. If you have ever watched my video on YouTube about my morning routines, you will see that I spend about 30 minutes each day meditating. I go to a quiet space in my house, do some deep breathing, and clear my mind. The purpose for this is to train my mind to stay calm and focused throughout the day. The value of this is that it makes it easier to stay in the moment when I'm doing something.

Let me give you some examples. Imagine that you are sitting down to complete your homework. You pick up your pencil and start working. Within 5 minutes, your mind is already wandering. Thoughts immediately start running through your mind about what you are going to eat for dinner, the post updates and videos you are missing on social media, and text messages that you want to send your friends.

Another example would be times that you spend with your family. Imagine that you are sitting at the dinner table and everyone is talking. Instead of engaging in the conversation, you are thinking about your homework, what you are going to wear the next day, and the time your favorite show is coming on TV that night. In both of these instances, you were physically present, but your mind was somewhere else.

You will miss out on memories, events, and relationships throughout your life if you don't stay present and in the moment. This is a really unique moment in your life. You are able to live with your parents for free, have all your needs paid for, and save as much money as possible. If you miss the opportunities that are given to you during this time of your life, you won't get it back. The same is true for every phase of your life. When it comes, you must take every opportunity in that moment so it can prepare you for the next moment.

The concept of staying in the moment is a difficult one to grasp. If you ask your parents, I'm sure they will list some regrets they have because they didn't enjoy the moment. We are still young, which means there are so many things that we have yet to experience. However, don't rush your current experiences to get to the next one. For instance, one day you will drive a car, but don't rush the luxury of being driven around by someone else. One day, you will own a home, but don't rush the experience of being able to live in a home for free.

There are many ways that you can practice staying in the present. One way that you can do this is through meditation. You don't have to do it for a long time, but you can start by doing 10 minutes every morning. I suggest that you do it before you go to school so that your mind can already be cleared. Get in a quiet space and play soft instrumental music in the background. While the music is playing, you can close your eyes and breathe deeply. The key here is to try to clear your mind without allowing your thoughts to go all over the place. Practicing this everyday will help your mind to learn how to stay focused and present.

Another thing you can do is keep a journal. Life can go by so quickly that we forget special moments. To keep you aware and mindful of the day's events, you can keep a daily journal that details the important moments. This is a great reflection activity, and it is something you can go back and read anytime you want.

Before I end this chapter, I have to go back to that song because every time I listen to it, I'm challenged to slow down and pay attention to my life. When life gets busy, I can rush through moments and forget about the important relationships in my life. I am then reminded that wherever I am, I must be there. When I'm interviewed at the ripe old age of 102, and I still have my good looks and bulging muscles (LOL!), I want to say that I didn't let my days pass by. I lived my life, met my goals, enjoyed success, traveled the world, cherished my family and friends, and changed the world.

I'm sure this is something that all of us would like to say, but it doesn't just happen. It means that you must stay in the moment. Celebrate every day of your life and don't be too anxious about what comes next. Don't spend so much time preparing for your future that you forget to live your present.

6

Don't be "Just a Kid"

One phrase that I encourage people to repeat all the time is, "Don't be average, be savage." The reason for this is that I want to destroy the phrase, "Just a kid." There are so many times adults will say, "Oh, you are just a kid," or "Why do you want to write a book? You are just a kid," or "Don't go after success because you are just a kid." If I could, I would erase the phrase from the human vocabulary.

The reason that I'm so passionate about this is because ever since I could remember, I've pursued the savage lifestyle. Why would you want to pursue anything else? Guys, a normal childhood is just that – normal. People that live normal lives don't have anything to brag about. Normal kids don't change the world because they are too busy being like everyone else.

The other day, it was unbelievably hot in Florida. It was one of those days that make you want to sit in a bucket of ice. I decided to go to the pool to cool off. When I got there, I noticed that there were two diving boards, the low one and the high one. The high diving board had a tall ladder leading up to the top. The height of the board was impressive and looked like an adventure. At the base of the ladder was a line of about 20 kids waiting their turn to dive off of it. Then, I looked at the low diving board. It was about level with the in-ground pool. There was not much about this board that was impressive or memorable. There was not one person in line to jump off of this board.

Do you know why there were so many people waiting to jump off the high board and not a single person waiting to jump off the low one? The answer is, no one cares about the low, but everyone cares about the high. The high board represents adventure, risk, and fun. When you jump off the high board, you create a splash that can be heard and felt. Everyone isn't willing to jump off the high board. Some people are scared because they feel like it may be too risky. On the other hand, the low board is easy. Anyone can jump off of it. It presents a low amount of risk and you barely make a splash.

This is similar to the average versus the savage life. Being, "just a kid," means that you are going to do what everyone else is doing. You won't have to take risks with your life. There will be very little adventure and excitement because you will be living the same way every other kid you know is living. The impact that you make with your life also will be small because the splash you make will only reach a few people.

The savage lifestyle is like the high board. The impact you leave when you refuse to be, "just a kid," will change the lives of so many other people. You will make a huge splash that will touch so many different lives. Everyone will not be willing to make the decisions you are making or take similar risks. This means that you will be living a life filled with adventure and excitement.

Think about kids like Justin Bieber, Chris Brown, Jake Paul, and Moziah Bridges. These kids represent singers, YouTube sensations, and successful entrepreneurs. They refused to settle for being, "just a kid." Moziah didn't let anyone tell him that he couldn't own his own bowtie line because he was just a kid. Justin Bieber didn't let anyone tell him that he couldn't be a pop star because he was just a kid. They absolutely destroyed that phrase from their vocabulary and jumped of the high diving board.

I remember during an interview someone asked, "Caleb, what would your life be like right now if you had decided to be, "just a kid.'" In response I said, "There is no average in my blood. Whatever path I chose to take, I would have gone after greatness." I didn't say this because it sounded good or I was trying to be cocky. It is the absolute truth.

When I wanted to be a magician, I watched YouTube videos, read books, and practiced juggling for hours. When I wanted to be a pro baseball player, I read books, watched YouTube videos of my favorite players, practiced daily, and completed drills as often as I could. When I wanted to excel in school I studied every day, completed my homework, and did extra assignments to sharpen my skills. Now that I'm an entrepreneur, I've taken that same savage mindset and put every part of me into my business.

It doesn't matter what I pursue, I will always seek to be savage. I will never settle for the average, low diving board. The world will hear and feel the splash from my life. That is who I was born to be. I know you guys are born to be that as well. Why? Because you are Maddix addicts.

7

Create Your Masterpiece

I'm going to tell you a story, and it is about you. Are you ready? You are sitting in a big, empty room with one large window in the far corner. Standing in front of a window is a huge blank painting. In front of the painting are 10 bottles of paint. Each bottle has a different, bright color inside. Next to the bottles are three different paint brushes. One is thick, the other is a medium size, and the third one is skinny. The different sizes are used to make different brush strokes.

Off to the side, is a stool. You walk up to the stool, take a seat, and grab the brushes and your first bottle of paint. I'm not going to tell you the color that you pick because it is your painting and your choice. As you grab your paint and choose the brush, you begin to fill the painting with color.

You continue painting for about 10 minutes. Suddenly, you notice people coming into the room behind you. They are your parents, coaches, teachers, friends, siblings, and other family members. The room that was once empty is now pretty crowded. The peace that you felt when you first started painting is beginning to leave as the soft noise of people behind you begins to get louder.

Trying to ignore the noise, you hear a comment come from the crowd. "Why did you pick that color? I think maybe red would have better to use in the right corner instead of yellow." Before you can respond, another voice follows the first. "Yeah. And why did you use the thick brush strokes at the top? The thin ones should go there, and the thick ones should be at the bottom."

The voices that were quiet at first now become rather loud and the comments that were only a few at the beginning were now coming from everyone in the room. There are different opinions offered based on your painting. Some people think you should have used more red. Other people think you should have used more blue. The noise becomes so loud that you can no longer focus on your painting.

Instead of completing your painting, you start to doubt what you have created and begin to make changes based on what other people are telling you to do. Here is the crazy part. Even after you make changes, people still aren't pleased because the comments never stop.

Moments later, you look at your painting and can no longer even recognize your creation. When you first started painting, you knew what you wanted it to look like. Now, you aren't even sure what you are looking it. It looks like a combination of what you started and the suggestions from everyone in the crowd behind you.

Why did I tell you this story? Because this is how many of our lives will look if we don't make the decision now to create our own masterpiece. I want you to think of the blank painting from the story as representing life. Sitting before you are years filled with choices and decisions that you have yet to make.

With each minute, hour, day, and year, your personal choices begin to fill that once blank painting.

Creating your own masterpiece can be such an amazing experience because you only get one life. You don't get to throw away your life and start a new one. What you are creating right now, you have to live with years from now.

Many times, when we are creating our masterpiece, we invite too many people into the room and allow them to determine what goes on our canvas. There is nothing wrong with asking for opinions and guidance. The problem arises when we depend on other people so much that we start to live our lives based on their opinions.

You can ask for help, but no one should be able to stop you from painting your masterpiece. Everyone is going to have a different opinion about who you are and what you should do with your life. Everyone is going to have different ideas about your choices and decisions. That is fine. As we talked about earlier, you can't control everyone's opinion of you, but you can make sure that their opinions don't control you.

One of the reasons that so many people can control our lives is because we don't really know who we are or what we are meant to do with our lives. That is ok. We are young, so we are slowly figuring those things out. But the goal is to discover who we are and what we are supposed to do with our lives. The same can be true for painting. You can't really create a masterpiece if you don't know what it is supposed to look like. You have to figure out what you are going to paint.

Once again, there is nothing wrong with guidance and mentorship. I encourage it. But there is a huge difference between guidance and control. If you are 100% sure about who you are and what you want to accomplish, you will attract people that want to support and guide you towards your goal. However, if you are unsure, people will come into your life and try to pull you in so many different directions.

Guys, I talk to adults all the time that told me that when they were my age, they had no idea what they wanted to do with their life. This meant that most of them started working jobs that they really didn't like, getting into relationships with someone they really didn't love, and making business decisions that cost them a massive amount of money. Most of them say that they sought the opinions of others to help them make their life choices.

How sad it will be to look at your masterpiece 10 years from now and not ever recognize what you created. In fact, if you allow everyone else to control your life, you can't even call it, "My Masterpiece," anymore. It will have to be entitled, "Everyone Else's Masterpiece." But it's not. This is YOUR life.

If I had asked my church leaders, friends, and coaches what I should do with my life, I would have received multiple answers. Why? Because they all have different opinions and perspectives about who I am and what I should do with my life. Henry Ford, the creator of the first automobile and Ford Motors said, "If I would have asked my customers what they wanted, they would have said a faster horse."

When I was at Arnold Schwarzenegger's house and I saw his accomplishments, I remembered a book I read that said his parents wanted him to see a psychologist because they thought his dreams were ridiculous. He wanted to become a world-famous body builder, but his parents believed that this was a crazy dream. If he had listened to his parents, he would not have achieved his goals or lived his dreams.

People are always going to have opinions about your life, both good and bad. I remember one time I was reading my messages on Facebook, and one popped up that said, "Caleb, your life is meaningless. No one cares about what you have to say. The world would be a better place if you just committed suicide." It is difficult for me to describe my thoughts after I read that message because I was in a state of shock. I couldn't believe that someone would be so cruel. That hurtful statement really impacted me. However, I could not allow the opinion of one person destroy my masterpiece.

I refuse to spend time trying to change the opinions of others. That is not my job. My job is to focus on my masterpiece and silence the voices behind me. Those present in my room of creation must be encouraging and supportive of my masterpiece. They don't have to agree with everything I do. That is unrealistic, but they do have to allow me to live my life without controlling me.

Each day, I choose to sit in front of that masterpiece and make another stroke and choose another color. I do it confidently because I know what I'm creating. Be on a constant search to discover who you are and what you want to do with your life. Create goals, get a clear focus, and create your life everyday. Remember, you only get one life so make it memorable. Make your masterpiece the one that gets hung in museums and sold for millions of dollars.

That's the value of my content. Each time you read, you are learning principles and values that will help you become a more genuine version of yourself. As you learn, you will begin to grow and discover who you are and what you want to do with your life. No one is going to have to force you to do it or give you the wrong information that will lead you down the wrong path. You will decide, and when you do, you will be able to create a masterpiece that you are proud of.

8

Message from Matt to the Parents

arents, let me ask you a question. Wouldn't it be absolutely amazing for your kids to enjoy their childhood and yet have a high level of success at the same time? You see, it is actually possible. I remember when I first got Caleb into reading success books, yoga, meditation, and taking him to feed the homeless. So many people kept cautioning me by saying, "Be careful. He still needs to be a kid." In fact, to this day, this is still the warning I get from people. They say things like, "Aren't you afraid that he is losing his childhood?"

I'll tell you my answer to these types of questions. I have not for one second had a fear about Caleb missing out or losing his, "childhood." His success, along with disciplines such as meditation, discipline, focus, and work ethic, have made his childhood even better. When you are focused and have a positive mindset that is added to work, it elevates confidence, mood, and overall self-perception.

The last thing we should be doing as parents is to allow people to put a fear in us that our kids are going to "miss out" on their childhood. I've always turned the questions back on my critics by asking, "Can you be a little clearer about the term 'childhood' that you keep referring to? Does this include playing video games all day until bedtime? Goofing off in class? Texting friends and staying on social media all day? Watching TV until their retinas burn?" Usually I'm still left with an unclear answer for what they mean by "childhood."

I believe the reason for this is because there are many people that have false, limiting beliefs about what it means to experience "childhood." Having said all that, my friends, I chose a long time ago to not give any time or attention to those that gave extremely negative feedback about my parenting decisions.

There are times when I will simply respond to the question, "Aren't you afraid that Caleb is losing his childhood?" with a short, confident response. To that I would say, "Absolutely, not. There is not one minute that I am afraid that he is missing out on his childhood." Once I complete that response, there is usually a quick moment of silence and that topic of conversation gets stopped dead in its tracks.

Caleb is 100% a kid. He may exhibit a greater level of maturity than other kids his age, but he is still a kid. He may be focused, disciplined, and have extreme work ethic, but he is still a kid. Parents, I want to encourage you. Just because you kid is 10-years-old, that does not mean they can't be more mature than other typical 10-year-olds. It also does not mean that they can't be focused, disciplined, motivated, and hard working. Also, just because your kid is 8-years-old doesn't mean that he can't desire to write his first book, become a social media star, or start his own business. Those desires don't negate childhood.

In fact, these characteristics and desires displayed in your child, show what an incredible job you are doing as a parent. You must stop caring about what other people think about your parenting style or decisions. You are the parent and you can allow your child to dream big, work hard, and achieve great things at a young age. You will have critics and those that demean your choices. That is ok. Allow your child to become the greatest human being on the planet without restricting him based on limiting, small-minded beliefs about "childhood."

I'm going to give you some of my best advice that will help you allow your kids to have success and still keep their childhood.

1. No limiting beliefs

I touched on this already, but I want to reemphasize that one of our primary roles as a parent is to instill the right beliefs within our kids. Yes, it's important that our kids don't cuss, earn good grades, show respect, and follow the rules. However, a higher level of parenting strives to train our kids to have strong, stable beliefs. We want them to believe in themselves, their dreams, unlimited possibilities, and that they can create and become anything they desire. We want to fuel their dreams and visions.

Look at your child's beliefs as a pile of wood, and we are the fire. As parents, we want to light their beliefs on fire with positivity and unconditional support. We are not going to allow limiting beliefs and limitations to dim the fire. We will not use phrases such as, "That's not possible" or "That is unrealistic." These phrases must be eliminated from our conversation if we are going to raise powerful kids.

2. Intentionally have fun and make memories

I'm a single parent and a business owner so needless to say, my schedule can be quite full. I know many of you can relate to this. Being busy and at times, overwhelmed, can be a reality for all of us. Despite this reality, it is so important to make time for your kids. This time must be intentional, fun, and memorable.

What good is money and success if you can't have fun and make memories? We found that the more successful we became, the more freedom we had to have fun and make memories. I want to stress something to some of you parents that may have children that will become famous actors, business owners, sports stars, etc. Increased success can also mean increased responsibilities and time requirements. In the midst of this, be intentional to have A LOT of fun.

Let your home be full of laughter and light-hearted humor. Caleb and I have a goal to make one memory every day. Whatever we have on our agenda for the day, we make sure that fun is implemented throughout. Make holidays fun and important. Start traditions, take pictures and videos, and constantly look for ways to make memories.

Fun, laughter, and memories help kids hold on to their childhood. It also teaches them to stay in the moment even with increased pressure and time constraints. Teach them the skill of enjoying and appreciating every moment.

3. Spend time with other friends

Caleb is a focused, hard-working young man. He enjoys spending time in the office working on his business and connecting with people. I encourage that. At the same time, I also understand the value of spending time with other kids his age. Even though I know Caleb could work all day everyday without taking a break, as a dad I have to teach my son balance. Part of that balance includes connecting with other kids his age.

I've studied many Olympic athletes and I was inspired by a gymnast named, Mary Lou Retton. She became an Olympic gold medalist when she was only 17-years-old. While this was a huge accomplishment, she had to pay a cost. At a young age, Retton started training for the Olympics which meant that she missed out on sleepovers, birthday parties, and school dances. Her success came at a price. While this is a principle of success, as Caleb's dad, I want to make sure that he still has the opportunity to interact with and have fun with friends.

This is the key, parents. I don't allow my son to hang out with negative, small-minded friends. His friends must be passionate, respectful, possess a high character, and have a desire for growth. Make sure your kids have a social life, but at the same time, monitor their friendships because this will make a huge difference in their overall success.

Remember, in our houses, the word, "average" is a sin. Average is blah, puke, and disgusting. They can train hard and work hard, but a social life that includes positive friends will bring a healthy balance to your child's life.

4. Set aside time blocks

I am proud of my son's motivation to work and achieve success. Like I said before, he is a hard-working young man. Each day, we set aside time for working. Once that time block is over, I tell Caleb to turn off his electronics and put his work away. During this block of time, he is not allowed to talk about business or strategizing. I want him to just be. I want Caleb to learn the art of being. It is a time when he doesn't have to be "on" or performing. It is not good for his brain to be in the nonstop mentality of push, passion, and work.

Actually, I have found that his productivity level rises when I shut everything down and let him rest. Don't get me wrong, there are seasons when we go hard for a longer period of time. We may be in a time frame that brings a heavy workload that requires 3 days of intense work.

The concept of time blocking is actually a great principle to teach your kids because it implements the importance of a schedule. If you break your kids' days into blocks of time, it will bring a greater focus and awareness of time. Also, it allows them a set goal to put their energy and focus into one or two actions at a time. Time blocking work, relaxation, play, technology, etc. can be a great tool to use so that your kids don't waste their time or become unbalanced.

Each day, I'll ask Caleb's his priorities for the day. Once we discover those, I block out time for each priority and hold him accountable to those time frames. I have found that Caleb is more focus, motivated, and gets more done when I use this approach. Balance is key to raising a successful kid that needs work time and play time.

5. Teach your kids to balance the core 4

The core 4 includes the physical, financial, relational, and spiritual aspects of life. As a family, we made a decision that we would never neglect these 4 areas of our lives. For example, there was a time when our family wanted to get together with us, but we needed to write our books that day. Because we committed to the relational aspect of our life, we had to remind ourselves that our relationships are just as important as our finances. Despite any deadline setback, we decided that spending time with our family that day was more important because of our commitment to balance the core 4 areas of our lives.

Parents, you must become intentional about your kids mastering the core 4. Your life will become progressively better. When your kids decide to take care of the physical aspect of their life, learn how to make and manage money, value the relationships in their life, and explore their spirituality, they will experience complete health in all areas of their lives.

I want to touch on the spiritual aspect for a moment because Caleb grew up going to church. I was a minister for many years, and as a teenager, he started to have his own questions and ideas about his spirituality. I was not upset about this because I always taught him to explore and search when it came to his spiritual beliefs. The biggest thing I taught was no matter what your beliefs, you must have daily spiritual practices. It doesn't matter how strong you are in the other three aspects of life, if you are lacking in one, your life will show the imbalance. I've always taught Caleb that it doesn't matter how successful you become, if your inner peace, happiness, and joy is lacking, it will diminish your success. With this truth, I've guided Caleb towards a number of spiritual practices as he continues to solidify his own spiritual beliefs.

Parents, I'm going to leave you with a challenge. As a mother or father, I really want you to start teaching and empowering your kids to be committed to those 4 areas of their life. Don't let them neglect those areas. Fulfillment is found in mastering and balancing these 4 areas.

The most important thing that you must remember when raising successful kids is that you must own your parenting style. It is not easy at times but stay the course. Decide how you want to raise your child. Use the tools given to you and your kids to help your kids grow and experience greater success. Your kid might not act like the other kids his age. He/she might think differently, talk differently, act differently, and dream differently. That's ok. That means that you aren't raising an average kid. Your kid is savage. This also means that you aren't an average parent. You are savage. Don't allow the average parents of this world rob you of the gift of raising your kids in an unorthodox way. Don't settle for the normal. Challenge your kids, encourage them, and follow the steps I've just given you to ensure that you have the balance necessary to raise a successful kid that still keeps their childhood.

Made in the USA
Coppell, TX
19 December 2019

13486668R10046